In less than a year, Boyzone have scored four Top Three hits in the UK and gone crashing straight into the album charts at Number One with their debut LP, 'Said And Done'.

The five Dublin boys have enjoyed success all over Europe and are national heroes in their home and of Eire. They have thrilled thousands on sell-out tours of the UK and Ireland, they have graced the covers of all of the major pop magazines - and now they have their very own OFFICIAL annual. They hope you'll have fun reading it, and learn more about Boyzone from it, because this is what it means to them.

It's a pleasure given you all info and I hope you enjoy reading it. Nice. Hope ☺ Shane

SHANE

Having our own annual is a very, very good feeling. I do remember saying 'When are we going to have our own song?' and 'When will we have a dance routine that we can dance to?' We've gone so far, to the point where we now have our own annual. I have to say that it's...un-bel-iev-able. It really is. For me this is just...out there! Hope you enjoy

Firstly I would like to thank all of our "Fans" no; I prefer to call you Friends, For supporting us in the way you have. What I have in Boyzone, Besides 4 great Friends, I have the chance to experience, An experience of a life time.. I wouldn't have that Without you guys "our Friends" Enjoy the Annual And I'll See you Soon Lots of love Always Keith xxxx

KEITH

Back home in Ireland, two people have already written books on Boyzone, so I'm kind of getting used to it now. But I'm glad that this annual is being printed because I didn't like the other books, and now I've got a say on what goes into the annual. I know it's not going to be rubbish - I know it's going to be straight from me. We're all often quoted saying things we never said, with this annual, at least, if I'm quoted saying something - then I know I've said it! That's a good aspect about this, and I hope you all like it.

I Would Just like to thank
All of you for your support
And helping to Achieve the
Success We have.
But on a personnal level
thank you for helping me
make my dream come true
I Love you

[signature: Michael Graham]

I'd like to say thanks to Everybody
for your support, your love, your kindness
Thanks for Staying with us.

lots of love + kisses
Best Wishes Always

[signature: Steve]

I'd like to take this time
to say thank you so much
for everything you've done for us
in the past and now in the
Present and, please God, in the
future

Thank for it all

God Bless

[signature]

CONTE

NTS

Written by Mike Hrano with Shane, Stephen, Mikey, Keith & Ronan.

Design by Louise Ivimy, Susan Bartram and Joanna Davies.

Published by Grandreams Limited Jadwin House, 205/211 Kentish Town Road London, NW5 2JU.

Printed in Italy.

STEPHEN ON SHANE: Shane is great, a really nice guy. He'll do anything for you; he's a caring guy. He's mad, in a sense, and he's very funny. He takes each day as it comes. If something happens, he says 'Oh, don't mind me. It's killed. Forget about it.' If you do something wrong, or forget to do something for him, he'll just go 'No problem, no problem.' He's just a very, very easy-going person. I get on very well with Shane, always have.

SHANE ON STEPHEN: Steve is very sensitive. If you say something that could hurt his feelings, he plays on that quite a lot. He's not an easy-going guy so far as that is concerned; he'll play on it all day. If he was to make a joke and you didn't laugh on it - he'll get hurt. He's a real strange bloke like that. If he taps you on the shoulder and he smiles at you, unless you smile back at him, he can get upset.

KEITH ON STEPHEN: I used to work with Steve in a shop before Boyzone began, so I know him pretty well. Stephen is most definitely the sensitive one of the band, anyone will tell you that. He can get a bit into himself sometimes, in the sense that he'll get moody or introverted, but he'll always snap out of it if there's something going on with the band that means he's got to - like a concert or something. He'll push aside his own feelings and just get on with the job in hand. In that respect, he's a true professional, and I admire him for that quality.

STEPHEN ON RONAN: Ronan's my best buddy in the band, I'm closest to him. He's just...so nice. A lovely guy, a caring guy. He's the one that sorts us all out. If there's plane tickets to get or if we have to be in the airport at such and such a time, Ronan's the person that'll ring you up and he'll get

TOGET

He gets annoyed. I've shared a room with Steve on many occasion, and he's great. He's fun to be around but, as I say, he is just that little bit sensitive about things from time to time.

STEPHEN ON KEITH: Oh, Keith! Keith is mad. Mad, mad, mad! Very funny, absolutely so funny. A headcase. He's the joker of the band, but if he wants to be serious, he can be very, very serious - and if he wants to be intelligent, or show his intelligence, he can. No problem. He's a very intelligent guy. He's great for a laugh, just a real joker, but he's sensitive, too. He can be very sensitive at times. If he wants to hurt a person, like if someone does something bad to him, he'll let that person know that they haven't done a nice thing. You know where you stand with Keith. He's a forward guy, and he'll tell you out straight what he thinks of you or if you've done something wrong. He's kind of like a spokesperson for the band; he sticks up and stands up for all or our rights.

you there. He'll tell you what time to be there at, tell you not to be late and make sure you bring everything you need. He's one of the most caring guys I know in the whole world. He'll do anything for you; he'll give you his last penny. If you're a friend of Ronan's, you're a friend for life. He'll always treat you as a friend. He's just a brilliant guy - anyone will tell you that. Everyone says it about Ronan; he's just a brilliant guy. He's so cool.

RONAN ON STEPHEN: Steve's the quiet one of the band. He has his own room when we're away. Shane and I share, and so do Mikey and Keith, but Stephen gets a room to himself. I think Steve prefers it that way, although there's no particular reason for him not sharing apart from the fact that five divided by two means that there will always be an odd one out who gets to have his own room. Steve is a very sensitive guy so, as I say, I'm sure it suits him to be on his own. I get on very well with Stephen. He's a good mate of mine, we were always mates from day one, and I love him a lot. We spend a lot of time together.

STEPHEN ON MIKEY: When Mikey and Keith get together ...awesome! There's no stopping the two of them from dossing. They just mess and mess and mess, but in a very funny way, like we get a great laugh out of them and all that. Mikey is a very mature person. Very, very mature - when he wants to be! He's very intelligent, too. He's got certain ways about him. If something is bothering him, he'll get straight to the point and make sure that he clears everything up. Or if he does something wrong on somebody, he'll say 'Right - what did I do wrong?' He'll sort things out there and then. He doesn't like dragging things on. He's sensitive, too. He's very close to his family and his friends and, again, if you're a friend of Mikey's, you're a friend for life. He can get very quiet, at times, and be very moody - he can be a moody

true little star, like. Definitely is.

SHANE ON KEITH: Keith is a very strange guy. When I say strange, I mean...he can be hard to work with because he doesn't care. It's not that he doesn't care, he's just...mad! He's just totally mad. He doesn't know when to stop. He can mess and mess and mess, and there's no stop or drawback to him. He just goes and goes and goes. And even if you're hurt in a certain way, feelings-wise, it doesn't matter; he just carries on. But then, changing it around, you cannot say diddly to him. Oh, my God! You say the slightest thing to him, and he's on a mad one. He's really, really strange like that; he gives so much - but he just cannot take.

KEITH ON SHANE: He's one of the nicest guys you could wish to meet. He's one of those fellows who seems to be

HER

NOBODY KNOWS BOYZONE BETTER THAN BOYZONE. HERE'S WHAT THEY HAVE TO SAY ABOUT EACH OTHER...

person, like myself - but he's a really nice guy. If you ever want to chat to him, he's there for you. He'll sit and he'll chat and he'll try and sort out your problems, even though he may have problems of his own.

MIKEY ON STEPHEN: Steve is a strange little character! Things get Stephen down quite easily, like when we're away from home an awful lot he gets down and quite upset and all. We just try and hold him together. The only thing about him is that, rather than let everybody help him and try and secure him, he kind of goes on his own - which isn't really a good thing. To us, anyway - because we're together a long time - he should open up. He does open up but, at times, he locks himself away. Which isn't right. But if he's in that sort of mood and goes on stage, he just completely turns around; he's all smiles, he's all dancing. You have to give it to him; he completely steals the show and takes it away - every night. Everybody loves him on stage. All the kids adore him. He's a

in one constant type of mood, and that mood is up and happy. He's not the sort of person to let things get to him, or get him down. That's just not his way. As a friend, he's reliable and you can depend on him; he'll be there for you if ever you need him. Of course, he's not as rowdy as me - but that's his problem! Mind you, he does like a laugh. The same as any of us. The other thing about Shane is that he's absolutely, totally mad about cars.

SHANE ON RONAN: The word 'together', well, that is Ronan - bar his hotel room, which is just a total mess. For knowing things and organising things, Ronan is The Man. He's Top Dollar, really is. He and I normally share rooms, and he's no trouble at all. He's a really great guy to be with and, with him around, you feel kind of safe. He'll always make sure that we are where we're supposed to be. He's possibly a bit too serious at times, for his age, but he likes a laugh the same as the rest of us.

RONAN ON SHANE: Shane is one nice guy. He so totally laid back about everything that he's almost not standing up. He never lets anything get to him or, if he does, he never lets it show. His attitude to a problem is always 'Don't worry about it, it'll pass.' That's a great way to be. He takes everything in his stride - apart from walls! (Editor's note: A cheeky reference to the fact that Shane broke his foot tripping over a wall...) Shane will do anything for you, he's a real mate, and he gets on with everybody. He's a happy-go-lucky bloke and he is great fun to have around. He's the sort of guy who'll lift you up when you're down - but he'll never be the cause of something that makes you feel bad. And he's absolutely mad for cars. He's the Damon Hill or Michael Schumacher of the band!

RONAN ON KEITH: Keith tries to be the funny guy of the band. Well, he is the funny guy of the band; he's very funny. He makes me laugh! He's a tough guy, you know, he's always digging people. He's always hitting you - and sometimes you feel like thumping the head off him. But there's no point, because he's bigger than me! Having said that, he's really not tough at all; he's got a heart of gold and he can be as gentle as the next guy. But you'd definitely want Keith on your side in a fight! He's a lovely guy. I love him, you know?

KEITH ON RONAN: You have to give it to Ronan; he's completely switched on. He knows where he's going, how he's going to get there - and what it will take to bring him to that place. He might be the youngest one in the band, but you'd never know it in a lot of ways. He's very committed to the band and to music, and has a real desire to find out as much about this business as he can. As a friend, you couldn't wish for a more generous, genuine and gentle guy. I think I get on his nerves from time to time, but that's just my way. I don't mean to, because I love him a lot.

a good or a bad thing, but I think he should learn to be an 18-year-old sometimes - rather than be so much older than his age all of the time. But that's not a fault, necessarily.

SHANE ON MIKEY: Mikey is kind of strange in that you won't know what way he'll be thinking a lot of the time. In general, he's quiet. You know, he doesn't start rows. If somebody is to say something to him, he doesn't snap back at you. He'll just go 'Yeah, yeah' and let it flow over him. He's not really a rowdy kind of bloke, although he can be, mind you, at times. He gets quite annoyed in the mornings. Morning time just does not agree with Mikey. He is sore! Once it comes to morning and he's cranky, that's it; you say nothing to him because he'll just click and he's on a mad one. On the other hand, he can be a real joker. He certainly has his moments. In fact, in general, he usually tries to be a joker.

MIKEY ON SHANE: Shane is a very quiet fellow. He has a good heart. He's a good guy, he doesn't interfere with anybody and he's very easy to get along with. He likes a laugh, as we all do, but he has an even temperament - so he's never too over the top, one way or another. He's not an easy guy to wind up because he doesn't seem particularly bothered or troubled by a lot of things that might get the average person going. He's pretty relaxed and takes things as they come. He's a nice guy.

RONAN ON MIKEY: Mikey and Keith are in the same boat; the two of them are always joking and having a laugh. Mikey sometimes has a more serious head on him than Keith - he knows when to stop and get work done. Keith is always laughing, but he knows, too, when it's time to work. Mikey, being the oldest member of the band, is obviously a mature type of person and it is sometimes difficult to figure out where he's at. But he's always there for you - and when he goes off on one of his funny moods, there's nobody funnier.

MIKEY ON RONAN: Ronan is the youngest in the band, he's only 18 years of age, but he's very well together. His head is very well together. He's one of the nicest guys you could know - he wouldn't say a bad word about anybody. He's a very genuine type of fellow. The only thing I fear about Ronan, for his own sake, is that he may be a little bit too old for his age. I don't know whether that's

MIKEY ON KEITH: Keith is the type of person that could be your greatest friend - and your worst enemy. He's a great bloke. He's serious at times - when things need to be serious - and he's a messer at the best of times. I'm not trying to outline faults or anything, but Keith doesn't know where to draw the line sometimes with messin' and carrying on. He's mad, and that's all there is to it.

KEITH ON MIKEY: Since I share rooms with Mikey, I think I probably know him the best out of all the guys in the band. He's a very loyal person, very caring, and he'll give you all the time in the world if you have a problem to bring to him. He can be a bit unpredictable in the sense that you never really know what kind of mood he's going to be in, from day to day. One minute he's matching me with the messin', the next he's quiet and serious. But, either way, he's never do anyone any harm. If he's a friend of yours, then you're a fortunate person. Oh, and he snores...

THE FATHER AND THE SON

If there's one thing that all the members of Boyzone feel equally passionate about, it's their families. Of course, that makes life particularly tough for them; being away from home as often as they are, the guys don't really get as much time together with their parents or brothers and sisters as any of them might like. Which probably makes them even more devoted, as you are about to read...

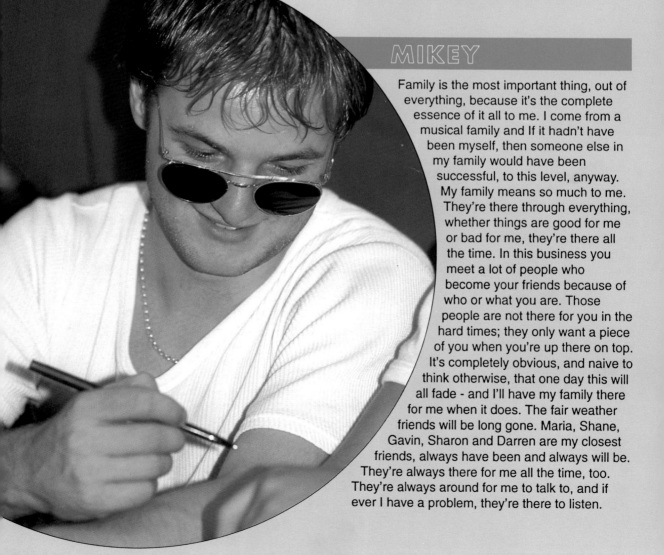

MIKEY

Family is the most important thing, out of everything, because it's the complete essence of it all to me. I come from a musical family and If it hadn't have been myself, then someone else in my family would have been successful, to this level, anyway. My family means so much to me. They're there through everything, whether things are good for me or bad for me, they're there all the time. In this business you meet a lot of people who become your friends because of who or what you are. Those people are not there for you in the hard times; they only want a piece of you when you're up there on top. It's completely obvious, and naive to think otherwise, that one day this will all fade - and I'll have my family there for me when it does. The fair weather friends will be long gone. Maria, Shane, Gavin, Sharon and Darren are my closest friends, always have been and always will be. They're always there for me all the time, too. They're always around for me to talk to, and if ever I have a problem, they're there to listen.

They're very good friends. You go through life and you meet many acquaintances, but only have one or two good friends. I'm just lucky that, outside of my family and the four good friends I have within the band, I've grown up with those other five. And they see me as me - not as a pop star.

STEPHEN

My family are right behind me in everything I do. I, for one, was never forced by my parents to go down a path that I didn't want to follow. They've always just let me choose my own way, because they only ever wanted me to be happy in my choice. It's quite difficult to talk about my family, actually; they mean that much to me. There's absolutely nothing more important in the world to me than my family. They're everything to me. Words just cannot describe. Family is a major issue in a country like Ireland, and in a city like Dublin, and all of us in the band come from a fairly large or large families. And we're all from happy families. We might not have come from wealthy backgrounds, but we come from stable homes filled with love and laughter. So we all know what a wonderful thing it is to have a good mum and dad, and good brothers or sisters. It's why Boyzone is a family in itself, in a way; we all appreciate that feeling of togetherness, belonging and support.

RONAN

I'm very close to all of my family. My eldest brother, Kieran, is married - Ann-Marie is his wife, and she's part of the family, too. They have two children, Conal and Rory - two good Irish names! - and Conal is my Godchild. Rory was just born in August, 1995. My sister Linda lives in New York, and she just sold shares in a restaurant and wants to go into the insurance business. She lives in Manhattan and works on Wall Street. Gerard works in the Stock Exchange on Wall Street. He's doing very, very well. Then there's Gary, who's in college in New York, studying foreign trade. And then there's moi! How come so many of my family are in New York. Well, Kieran was the first. He got up and left Ireland because there were no opportunities for him at that age. He went, Linda followed then Gerard then Gary. I'd be there now, too, if it wasn't for Boyzone. I was left on my own for a long time at home. Family is very, very important. I don't know what I'd do without them. They're very supportive. I have four guys here in Boyzone who are my brothers, as well, and we are very strong together, which is great. But you also need your own family when you go home. My

Mum and Dad are very important to me. They're very strong and supportive and proud of me, which means a lot. All of my family are very proud of me. It's fantastic.

KEITH

I come from a very close-knit family. We're extremely close and we're always there for each other. They have given me such tremendous support in my life, and my parents have always encouraged me in whatever it was that I wanted to do. My family mean the absolute world to me, being quite honest with you - and without their backing in all of this, it wouldn't be worth it. They're proud of me, they know I work hard, but my mother and father are proud of all of us. They wouldn't be more proud of me than anybody else in the family. My elder brother is a civil engineer, he's a site manger, and my younger brother is studying for his final year in school. They're very proud of all three of us, there's no special treatment for me or anything like that. Which is exactly as it should be.

SHANE

Like everyone else in the band and, hopefully, everyone in general, my family is very important to me. Your family is a major force in the way you are, the way you turn out, and I have every respect for my parents. I don't think they did too bad a job on me. My father works really hard and, for two months of every year, he goes over to a place we have in Portugal to relax. I've had some great times over there, we all have, although it's not so easy now for the whole family to be together there in the way we used to. As you grow up and get a job, you maybe can't afford two months off. I think the whole of my family is as pleased with my success in Boyzone as I am.

PERSONAL FILES
STEPHEN

● **FULL NAME:** Stephen Patrick David Gately.

● **DATE OF BIRTH:** 17.3.76.

● **PLACE OF BIRTH:** Dublin.

● **BIRTHSIGN:** I'm a Piscean, and I'm sensitive and emotional.

● **HOME:** Right in the city centre of Dublin.

● **FAMILY:** Mum and Dad, Margaret and Martin, three brothers - Mark, 25, Alan, 21, and Tony, 14 - and one sister, Michelle, 23.

● **PREVIOUS JOBS:** I worked in a bar in Dublin, but I won't mention the name because they weren't very nice to me so I don't want to give them any publicity! I worked in a theatre, the Olympia Theatre, in Dublin. That was good, I liked that. I stacked up all of the glasses and bottles, and made sure that everything was in the fridges. It was a good job. I was the only person in the building because I started at 7am, finished at 2pm - and had the rest of the day to myself. And the money was good! Then I had a job in a clothes shop, one of the big fashion clothes shops, in Dublin; McKullus. They did really, really nice stuff - all the top names - and I enjoyed it there. The shop is still open.

● **SCHOOL DETAILS:** I went to three schools, all within five minutes of my house, and I never had to wear a uniform - which was great as well. I loved secondary school, I got on well with all of the teachers. I loved school full stop; when you're in school you're just dying to get out, but once you leave you realise that it was a great time and great fun to be there. Sometimes I miss it, and sometimes I go in to see my old teachers. My primary school was St. Lawrence O'Toole's, senior boys school was St. Lawrence O'Toole's CBS and the secondary school was the North Strand Vocational School.

● **QUALIFICATIONS:** I got a few. I got my Cert, and I did a lot of Honours - which is like the equivalent to 'A' Levels. I got an 'A' grade in Honours Science and Honours English, and 'B's and 'C's in other subjects.

● **HEIGHT:** 5ft 7ins.

● **WEIGHT:** 9.5 stone.

● **SHOE SIZE:** I'm a 7. Small feet...

● **FAVE NIGHT OUT:** To the cinema, followed by something to eat and then to a bar. After that, back home and to bed.

● **FAVE NIGHT IN:** I love nights in. That's a brilliant thing for me. When I do get a night staying in, I love just getting out a couple of videos to watch, having a few drinks and then, after that, ordering a Chinese and relaxing in front of a great big fire.

● **FAVE MOVIE:** Casper. I loved it; it was a brilliant movie. And I'm just a big kid.

● **FAVE ACTOR:** Brad Pitt.

● **FAVE ACTRESS:** Julia Roberts.

● **FAVE SONG:** One of my favourite songs of all time is the song 'It's A Wonderful Life' by the group Black.

● **FAVE BAND:** I'd have to say my buddies, my friends; Deuce. They're great.

● **FAVE SINGER:** Probably Janet or Michael Jackson.

● **FAVE ALBUM:** At the moment, it's the Michael Jackson album 'HIStory.'

● **FAVE FOOD:** Chinese.

● **FAVE DRINK:** Probably water.

● **FAVE TV PROGRAMME:** Top Of The Pops. But, no, I never thought I'd one day appear on it. Never, never, ever, ever, ever...

● **FAVE COLOUR:** Blue.

● **CAR:** I don't have a car, and I can't drive! I'm the only one in the band who can't.

● **HOBBIES:** Don't have time for hobbies! I like going to the cinema, and I also like swimming - although I haven't been for a while. I also likex being with my friends, if you could call that a hobby! But I don't collect stuff, or anything like that.

● **AMBITIONS:** Just to be successful. At the end of the day, I love this band and I want to be with it for as long as I can - for as long as people buy our records.

So Good!

Sure, there's a lot of hard work to be done if you're a member of Boyzone – but it's not all bad news! We asked the guys what's so good about being in the band...

Shane:

The best bit about being in Boyzone is that I have four lads that I can rely on. Four really good friends in the band that would do anything for me. I think what tops it all off, even though we do a lot of hard work, is going out on stage. We do lot of interviews - and I don't consider them hard work because I quite enjoy them - and a lot of photo sessions and TV appearances, all of which involve a lot of waiting around. And

sometimes you do think 'What am I doing all of this for?'. It kind of gets you down a bit, but then when you go out on stage and you perform to people that really want to see you - and you know you're making them happy - it's just...I don't know, it's unbelievable, really. The rush you get when you go out on stage and hear them screaming for you, it's really, really strange. It's also the greatest feeling.

opportunities to travel and do things which you just wouldn't get in the normal 9 to 5. You have to make the most of those opportunities and see them for what they are; there while the going is good. Because there is a downside to all of this, of course. First of all, you can never know how long everything that's so good about Boyzone is going to last. At the end of the day, if the fans aren't buying our records and making hits out of them, then there's nothing. There's a downside to everything, but nobody sees it. The downside is leaving home so much, not seeing your friends and family. As I say, because I've spent 18

years of my life in Ireland - and I'm only a young lad, like - going away from my Mam all the time, not seeing my mother, is hard. And you don't eat the right food when you're travelling, you don't get enough sleep, nobody treats you with respect - you get no respect at all from a lot of people. Which is very hard, because we do work hard and when you don't get respect it just makes you feel like 'That's it - I've had enough.' It's tough sometimes. You pass into the public domain and people think they own you. They don't realise you're a human being, flesh and blood. They think you're just a robot, superhuman, that can take all of this. They don't realise how soft and sensitive people are or how human people can be..

Ronan.

For me, what's so good about all of this is the travelling, going and meeting new people, having a laugh, going to the parties...just having a good time and enjoying yourself. Being in Boyzone, we're getting

Steve.

One of the best things about being in Boyzone is the travelling. We're getting to see the world. And when you do go to places, because you're in a group you're treated a lot better - and with a lot more respect in some cases, in some countries. That can be very nice. But the best thing about being in Boyzone is...your dream. There's a possibility of your dream coming true at the end of the day - a very strong possibility. There's a lot of good things about being in Boyzone, like we meet all of these people. You meet so many

people...all these other acts. I mean, there's acts out there that I said I'd love to meet a few years ago, and here I am now on stage, singing with them. It's crazy. It's hard to believe. Coming from where I'm from. You know, I don't come from the richest of places, I come from a very poor place in Dublin. Nobody pushed me into doing anything I didn't want, and nobody pushed me into acting or singing. I just pushed myself, luckily. I'm glad I did, anyway. It's turned out brilliantly for me.

Mikey:

It is so good because, me being a little bit older than the rest of the lads, I've seen a little bit of life before the band - so I have something else to compare it with. I left school, after completing my leaving certificate, obviously before they did and I've worked in jobs. I know what it's like trying to survive having to work from Monday to Friday and having to get up out of bed and go to work - rain, hail or snow. Not that I had incredibly hard times or really suffered, but it was hard enough for me to feel the pinch, to appreciate how difficult it can be when you have very little money and yet you have to make that money stretch a long way. Of course, times have changed. Things are just as hard, but in a different way. Now what's tough is the fact that we have to work so hard, but money is no longer the issue that it was. That makes a tremendous amount of difference, and takes the pressure off, but I believe I do know what it's like to be without the potential for endless opportunity or to not have the world as your oyster. I often think about how my life would have continued had it not been for Boyzone. I know I would have still been happy, but my circumstances and the kind of life I would have led would have been worlds apart. Boyzone has given me some stability -plus, of course, all of the things which I'm sure all of the other guys have already mentioned; success, fans - and the four incredible friends in the band.

Keith:

You're put on this earth, right? And you're born and you're sent to school and you can meet, say, 30 other people - boys or girls - in your class, none of whom you know. So you're given the opportunity then to make your personality, and make you sense of humour. Everybody has these things, but it takes more to bring it out in some people than others. When you get into situations like that, when you have to live with other people that you don't know, that's when you start building your actual person. Now, you can make loads of friends in school, and you'll start making some outside of school when you go out at night, maybe, as you're getting a little bit older. You're meeting people all of the time. The point is this; Boyzone has given me four true friends. I've said this before, one or two times, but you can go through life and you can always have 15 mates on the street corner. You can hang around with them, stay where you are for your whole life and never make anything of yourself - but how many of those 15 mates are your real friends? If you go through life and maybe if you meet one or two really, really good friends - well, you're doing alright, you know? What Boyzone has given me is four other blokes that I live, sleep and do everything with and, thank God, we all get on very well and, to me, those guys are my brothers. I'm lucky in the sense that I'll never want for anything in love or in relationships with friends because I have four guys that I know will always be there for me and will always stand up for me. That's something that you can't ask for and you can't plan to go out and want to get. You're just given it. Money can't buy it. That, to me, means the world. To know that I'm not ever going to be lonely in this life. God forbid, when my family are gone I know I'll still have my good friends - and that's the four guys in this band. To me, you can't top that. You can't buy that. Boyzone has given me an awful lot more, of course, but the basic thing that's so good about this is that I've got four good friends that I really, really thank God for.

boyzone

play a very active part in their fan club and its magazine. The 24-page BOYZINE MAGAZONE is published every three months and features exclusive interviews with the band, specifically for the fans. It's only available to members, and if you would like further information about it and Boyzone's only OFFICIAL international fan club, then send a stamped, self-addressed envelope (or an International Reply Coupon if you're living outside of the UK) to:

**boyzone FAN CLUB,
P.O. BOX 102,
STANMORE,
MIDDLESEX,
HA7 2PY,
ENGLAND.**

The BOYZONE FAN CLUB HOTLINE is the OFFICIAL telephone information service for Boyzone. It's up-dated at least once a week with all the latest news about the band, and you can call it now on:

☎ **0891 81 81 03**

(Calls are charged at 49p per minute peak rate, and 39p at all other times. Please get permission from the person paying the bill before you make a call).

Please note: At present,
the BOYZONE FAN CLUB HOTLINE
can only be accessed by
callers living in the UK.

THERE'S NO QUESTION ABOUT IT; THOUSANDS OF GIRLS THINK THE GUYS IN BOYZONE ARE PERFECT. BUT WHAT KIND OF GIRLS DO THE GUYS GO FOR AS AN IDEAL PARTNER? WITH GREAT BIG GRINS ON THEIR FACES, THEY TOLD US...

STEPHEN: Personality counts and, to me, looks count, too. Some people say that looks don't matter, but I think they are important in a person. A girl doesn't have to be brilliant looking or absolutely beautiful...she just has to be nice. Everyone has beauty in a certain way. I like a girl...any type of hair, that doesn't matter. As long as she's friendly, with a good personality and is a bit good-looking, then that's what I'm after. There are girls that go out and see us and they just scream, but they only want us for being in the band. They don't know me as Steve - the real Steve. They just know me as Steve from Boyzone, so you wouldn't know whether to go out with people like that or not. But there is a possibility that you could go out with a fan. I could, I know I could - it's just a matter of seeing the right one. Girls are great, I love girls. And I like a girl for being herself, not for putting on an act in front of me and saying

that she's something else, or she's this and that. I like a girl to be up straight; if she's from a poor family, then that's no problem. I like a girl to be honest and truthful, rather than on the first date have her say 'Oh, you know, my Dad owns this company...' That's not on. I like a girl to be herself - and I do like brown-haired girls with brown eyes. And I like dark, dark-skinned girls.

KEITH: The main thing for me in a girl is her personality. She has to be a nice type of person, who's honest and true. I'm not into people who put on airs and graces, or find it hard to be natural. If you're not being natural, you're not being yourself. The other crucial thing in any relationship I have is that the girl must be able to accept the fact that, because of my job, I'll be away from her and from my home very often. And sometimes I'll be away for

RONAN: My ideal girl? I don't know. I haven't really got an ideal girl, to be honest with you. Everywhere you go in the world there's different people, different races and the spice of life, you know, variety, is important. I don't go out there looking for a certain type of girl, with blonde hair and green eyes or brown hair and brown eyes. Variety is the spice of life. I like a girl to be herself. That's what I like; for her to be herself with me and not try to be somebody that she's not, because that's so false and a real turn-off. It's disgusting. I do like a natural girl, as well. I don't like girls dolled up and all that crack. I just like a nice normal girl.

weeks on end. So it's absolutely essential that a girl I'm in a relationship with can trust me, and that I can trust her. I want any girl in my life to be waiting for me when I come back from travelling, knowing that everything is alright and that I haven't messed around on her and that she hasn't messed around on me, either. I also look for someone I can go out with and never be short of conversation with. There's no point being with someone you can't talk to. Even if what you're talking about is not of real interest to your partner, you should at least be able to discuss it to an open ear. Of course, looks are important - you can't see personality from across a room, afterall. But, at the end of the day, it's not whether a girl is gorgeous or whether she's ugly; it's what's inside that counts. I know a lot of people say that and don't mean it, but I genuinely do. I have to say that I would prefer to go out with a good-looking girl, but I don't have any preference in hair colour or anything like that because there's so many different types of gorgeous girls with all different colours of hair. I like green eyes, but I wouldn't mind if they were blue or brown, either! I can't really pinpoint my ideal girl down to one type of girl because there's so many types of beautiful and very nice ones around...

the day, her knowing that I'm actually taking care of her and I'm looking after her. A taller girl does intimidate me. I feel too insecure about being beside a taller girl or a bigger girl. I don't know why, but it just makes me feel that she's just totally overpowering. Eye colour doesn't matter whatsoever with me. Personality-wise with a girl, I'm not into loud girls whatsoever. I like a girl who's...not shy, but who doesn't mouth out about things. Someone you can have a decent conversation with; she'll laugh at your jokes and she'll make you laugh. Someone I can get on well with. I definitely don't go for a personality clash. A girl has to be...not different to me, but into different things. Then I can get together with that girl and teach her what I like to do and watch, and likewise. That way, if she's not interested in what I do, she's not interested - we'll move on to the next thing. At least I'll feel good about myself that I have shown her.

SHANE: Qualities I look for in a girl, eh? Well, definitely I don't look for a particular kind of girl in terms of hair colour, body or all of those things that people might go for. The one thing that has to be, for me, is that she has to be small. I just cannot cope with a taller girl. A girl has to be around chest height to me. For me, personally, I have to have a small girl because then I feel like I can take care of her. To hug her, I can get my arms all the way around. She feels much closer to me because I can take more of her in my arms, or what have you. I like a girl to look after me but I prefer, at the end of

MIKEY: The bottom line is, if I first meet a girl then, obviously, I have to feel attracted to her. So if she's an attractive looking girl to some degree, then that's a great start. However, what I might think is really beautiful, someone else might think is really ugly! As they say; beauty is in the eye of the beholder. If the girl is attractive to me, then I'd just like her to be down to earth, who has a nice personality and who I feel I would do anything for - die for, eventually - and who would do the same for me. A relationship is very, very important to me. Honestly...

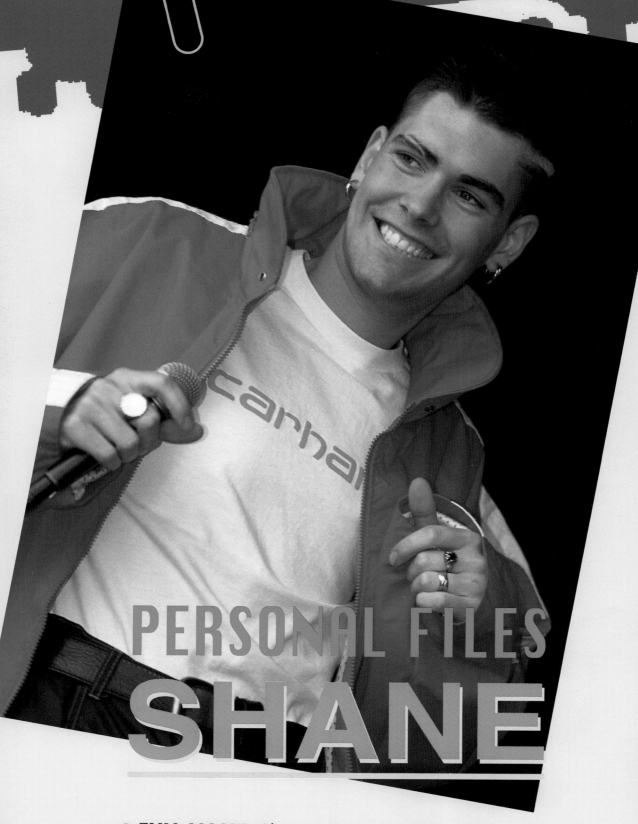

PERSONAL FILES
SHANE

● **FULL NAME:** Shane Eamonn Mark Stephen Lynch.

Is it Stephen with a 'ph'? To be quite honest...I don't know! I was Christened Shane Eamonn Lynch and then, for Confirmation, you have to choose another name that you wish to have. So, basically, I liked Mark and I liked Stephen...and I just picked them two. You can pick as many names as you want for your Confirmation.

● **DATE OF BIRTH:** 3.7.76.

● **PLACE OF BIRTH:** Dublin.

- **BIRTHSIGN:** Cancer. Do I have any of the characteristics of a typical Cancerian? Haven't a clue!...

- **HOME:** I live in Dublin with me Ma and Da.

- **FAMILY:** Mum and Dad, Noelene and Brendan, and five sisters. My eldest sister is Tara, 23 - she has her son, Dean, who is my nephew and my Godchild - the next sister down would be Alison, 20. She works in a computer factory or something. She's a yuppie, anyway! I have two younger sisters, who are twins; Keavy and Edele. They've just done their Inter and they've left school now, and they want to go forward with their dance career. They actually danced on a Boyzone tour we did in Ireland. They danced with our support act. And then I have my youngest sister, Naomi, 12, who's just going into Secondary now.

- **PREVIOUS JOBS:** When I was going to school, I worked in a petrol station, for two years. After that, I went on in the same garage and I became a mechanic for another two years.

- **SCHOOL DETAILS:** The first school I went to, Santa Sabina, was actually an all-girls' school! Up to your Major Communion, I think, it was mixed but it was all girls after that. I left that school before they made me wear a dress! Then I went to an all-boys' school, St. Bridget's, until my Sixth Class. From there I went on to Secondary school, to Grange Community College, and I was there until the third year - and then I left school.

- **QUALIFICATIONS:** I did what's called my Inter, or Junior Cert. I got three honours and five passes. Which is quite good. Well...it's quite good for me because I really didn't expect to pass because I went into school with one copy for each subject. I didn't even go in with books. I had a copy, and a pen and I just didn't do anything at school. I had no interest whatsoever. All I was waiting for was to get home and get out on my motorbike.

- **HEIGHT:** 6ft.

- **WEIGHT:** 11.5 stone.

- **SHOE SIZE:** 9.

- **FAVE NIGHT OUT:** Racing cars.

- **FAVE NIGHT IN:** In front of a fire, on a big sofa - with a girl and some popcorn - watching a video.

- **FAVE MOVIE:** Point Break.

- **FAVE ACTOR:** Brad Pitt is pretty smooth.

- **FAVE ACTRESS:** Now, my favourite actress used to be Melanie Griffiths, because I just thought she was really nice and I like an older woman. But I think I'll have to go off her now, for Drew Barrymore.

- **FAVE SONG:** I'll tell you one song I always loved; You Got Me Spinning by The Bass Pumpers. That is just a wicked track.

- **FAVE BAND:** I don't actually have a favourite band. The music I listen to is usually black music. I like Public Enemy quite a lot, but there's a lot of other bands I like which are up there with them. Public Enemy is just the first one I can think of, off the top of my head.

- **FAVE SINGER:** No particular favourite.

- **FAVE ALBUM:** I don't have a favourite album.

- **FAVE FOOD:** Most definitely shellfish. Lobster is top dollar!

- **FAVE DRINK:** I don't really have a favourite. If I haven't drunk milk in a long time, then that is my favourite drink for a while. Whatever I haven't had for a while, I long for for a few weeks and then I go off it and go on to another drink. I very, very seldomly drink alcohol. Only really on occasions like Christmas, and so on.

- **FAVE TV PROGRAMME:** I like to watch a programme called RPM. It's about cars, usually to do with rallying. Or else Top Gear is quite good sometimes.

- **FAVE COLOUR:** Black.

- **CAR:** A 911 Porsche.

- **HOBBIES:** Racing cars, water skiing, jet skiing - and I love off-road motorbike racing. I'm a bit of a speed freak, me. I think flying is the next thing for me, although I have flown already.

- **AMBITIONS:** Well, I could have said 'A Number One album' but, as we've achieved that...it would be to play at Wembley Stadium.

LOVE ME FOR A REASON

Ask the guys in Boyzone what has made all their success possible, and they will instantly give you a four-letter word as an answer; F.A.N.S. Boyzone spell out the message loud and clear; fans have given them everything, and without fans the group would be nothing. Here's what else they had to say about the kind of people reading this annual...

STEPHEN: Fans...the fans are great. Without them, where would you be? They're the ones that meet you at the airport and at the hotel to give you a welcome. They're the ones that buy albums - annuals. They are everything. They are our everything. The fans can be fantastic, and I've got to know a lot of them. I've got to know some of them by name, which is good on their behalf as well as mine; I can address them by their names which, hopefully, pleases them. Fans are lovely, really nice. In foreign countries, as well, they're great. If you have a fan, they'll support you. Every single day of the band, you're meeting fans - every single day - so, of course, there is a time when you'd like a break. Sometimes you'd like to say 'I'd wouldn't like anyone to come near me today. I'd just like to go out on my own, and walk around...' Which isn't really possibly any more. There's times when I wish that I could have days like that because being stressed, being tired and run down can be very hard on you. At those points, and in those moments, you do need to just rest. If there are fans there, you don't really have that much time to rest - which we don't mind, because we rest at night time. But if you want a

quiet day out or anything like that, it's kind of impossible. To have a fan club, though, is...mad! We've got names and addresses from more than 30,000 people who have written into our fan club. 30,000 people! What can you say? All those people sending in letters and presents...it's crazy. There's no other word for it. But it's great, absolutely brilliant. I'm so pleased with it, and it shows you how much support the fans give us.

SHANE: The view on fans for me, I suppose, is that fans are what make you, right? I wouldn't be sitting here now, being interviewed for this annual, if it wasn't for the fans. Although they know everything about your life, as far as I'm concerned, that's my job. That's what I have to do. If the fans want to spend time with you, you have to give it to them. Of course, sometimes you can't spend time with them because you have to go and do something. Although the fans might not understand that, and they might call you this, that and the other because you didn't stop and talk, it sometimes really isn't possible. Maybe 70% of the time it isn't possible, because you are rushing around and doing a lot of things, and I know the fans don't realise that - but it's also hard for us to cope with it when they call us names because we can't stop! But I just think that the fans are totally brilliant in general, and I think it's really excellent that they are supporting us and doing all that for us. Because we didn't really know what to expect when we started off singing and dancing - we didn't know where we'd get - and the fans have been totally supportive for us. The fans have just made us. That's the way it is...

RONAN: The fans are brilliant. They're the ones who support us and meet us and follow us and give us presents...I don't know how they do it, to be honest with you, because I don't know if I would be able to. You have to give them so much time, that's so important, because they make you. Wherever we go, they're always there for us. Sometimes it can be hard to give them what they want, though. If you give some fans too much time then they think they own you, if you give them too little time then they think that you don't care. It's very hard; you have to take a step back and strike the right balance with the fans. It's very hard to judge because if they think they own you and you don't come out, then they get very upset and that's even harder for you. Then they might leave you and not buy your records...it's a vicious circle. But we all try to do our best. We all try to give as much to the fans as we possibly can. The thing is, from day one the fans have been right behind us 100% - in terms of the fan club, in particular. Having a fan club is very important for everyone and, although we personally are not able to reply to the letters sent in ourselves, they are read and, where appropriate, they are responded to. We're told our fan club is going to be a very large one and, please God, it will be. But we don't want to count our chickens before they hatch. We're just amazed that so many thousands of people have already joined.

MIKEY: The short and sweet of it all so far as the fans are concerned is that, without them, we are nothing. I know people would kill to be in this position, and it is an excellent position to be in - with all of the fans and so on - but it's an awful lot tougher on this side, now I know, than I had imagined when I was...an average guy. Believe it or not, I still am an average guy. I don't think that unless you're completely dedicated to this, and unless your heart and soul is in it, then you wouldn't put up with what you have to put up with. As for the fans who would kill to get near you...well, that's another issue altogether and strange in it's own way - but I'd be privileged if somebody wanted to tear a piece out of me! I know that Stephen and Ronan are more favoured in the band, anyway - like everybody always rushes to them first - and that doesn't really bother me too much, because I'm a bit older. But I'd be happy now if somebody wanted a piece of me! I'd try not to mind...

SHANE: What fans are, whether they be boys or girls, are people that - first of all - like the look of you and the sound of your music. Some get obsessed by you, some just like to stand back and watch you perform. Whatever the case may be, it's very weird and hard to get a grasp on other human beings idolising you in the way that they do. It's hard to come to terms with it, but if you think about it for too long...you'll just become totally confused. You're better off not thinking about it at all. And I don't like to address these people as 'fans'.

That's a bit too degrading for me; I prefer to call them friends. Because that's what they are. They're very nice people. They're there for us and, as much as it's possible, we try to be there for them. Of course, we can't always give everything to everyone that wants something - or give each of our friends all the time that they might like with us - but we do what we can. The other important thing to realise is that, although this whole thing might start with us, with Boyzone, it finishes with the people who buy our records...

RONAN

● **FULL NAME:** Ronan Patrick John Keating.

● **DATE OF BIRTH:** 3.3.77.

● **PLACE OF BIRTH:** Dublin.

● **BIRTHSIGN:** I'm a Piscean and I'm a very sensitive person which is a very big part of being a Pisces. A lot of them love water, which I do, but I'm afraid of the sea. So I don't really share that aspect of the starsign.

● **HOME:**
I live at home with my Mum and Dad in Dublin.

● **FAMILY:** Mum and Dad, then there's Gary, 23, Gerard, 26, Linda, 27, and Kieran, 30. I'm the baby.

● **PREVIOUS JOBS:** I worked with my Mum for a while at the hairdresser's she used to have, worked with my Dad on the trucks and then I worked for four years in a shoe store called Korkys. It's a big store in Ireland and my brother, Gary, worked there and he got me the job. That made me grow up a lot, working in there, because it was in town and I used to work there every Saturday, then I started working the summer, then the Christmases and, before I knew it, I was taking days off from school to go in and work! I was a bit of dosser; I needed money. I liked having money, and I got very fond of it. It's a good store, Korkys - and they give us all of our shoes free now.

● **SCHOOL DETAILS:** Oh, I've been around! Bayside National School, Dunsany National School, then back to Bayside, on to St. Vintants Secondary School, then to Dunshocklin Secondary School, back to St. Vintants - and now I'm in Boyzone Primary School. Or perhaps that should be Boyzone Infants School...

● **QUALIFICATIONS:** Passed my Inter Cert, my Intermediate Certificate - which is like

GCSEs, I guess - and then myself and Stephen were about to do our equivalent of 'A' Levels when we dropped out of school for the band.

● **HEIGHT:** 5ft 9ins.

● **WEIGHT:** 10st.

● **SHOE SIZE:** 9.

● **FAVE NIGHT OUT:** Going to a movie and going for a nice meal afterwards. That's what I love. That's my favourite.

● **FAVE NIGHT IN:** Sitting at home, watching a movie in front of the fire wrapped up in one of those deerskin rugs. With the rain beating against the window. Oh, perfect!

● **FAVE MOVIE:**
The Highlander Trilogy or State Of Grace.

● **FAVE ACTOR:**
Christian Slater and the late River Phoenix.

● **FAVE ACTRESS:** Sandra Bullock.

● **FAVE SONG:** I like a lot of songs, I'm a big ballad fan. I like 'Crying' by Roy Orbison, I'm very fond of that, and there's a country and western song, 'The Way You Love Me', by a guy called John Michael Montgomery, which is a great song.

● **FAVE BAND:** Probably Del Amitri.

● **FAVE SINGER:** George Michael.

● **FAVE ALBUM:** I like a lot of Motown, and the Motown compilation that was out early in 1995 was absolutely brilliant. I thought it was fantastic. I also like the latest album by an Italian singer called Eros Ramazotti.

- **FAVE FOOD:** Chinese.

- **FAVE DRINK:** Ice cold water.

- **FAVE TV PROGRAMME:**
Quantum Leap.

- **FAVE COLOUR:** Blue. It's a shade called lapis lazuli, and it was the very first colour. It's the most incredible blue you'll ever see. It's beautiful.

- **CAR:** BMW 318i.

- **HOBBIES:** I like listening to music, to be honest with you. I actually like classical music. I like just turning all the lights out in the house, sitting on my own in my armchair with some classical music playing and just chilling out. Because I don't have much time to do it, when I do do it, I try and do it as best as I can and just totally turn off! I also like cars. Rallying and all of that stuff.

- **AMBITIONS:** This is my ambition; what I'm doing. Just to be successful at this. I love being in Boyzone, it's my life, and I'd like to be as successful as I can with the band. Maybe a couple of Number One singles and Number One albums wouldn't go astray!

You've already read about what the guys think about each other, now find out what they think about... themselves!

STEPHEN: Steve is weird, he really is. I really am! I can be very serious at times, although I love messin', I love dossin', as well. I'm a caring person. I pity the least little thing, like if I see an old woman walking down the road I'll go 'Oh, look at her. God bless her...' I can be very shy and quiet at times. I'm unpredictable with my temper and my moods. Nobody can predict what mood I'm going to be in; one day you could see me and I could be really jolly, the next day I won't want to do anything, just lie there. I'd say I'm alright but, looks-wise, I don't see myself as a good-looking bloke at all. I've always said that. I've got a horrible body; I think that, too. People say I'm good-looking, and magazines ask me 'Of course you think you're good-looking! You have to think you are otherwise you wouldn't be in a band', and stuff like that. But I really don't know why. Ok, yeah, there is something there - but I don't think it's that much. I'm a very homely person. I love my home, I love my family and I love hanging around with mates. I'm just...I don't know. What else can I say about myself? I wear my heart on my sleeve and I'm a forward person in the sense that if I'm fed up with someone, I'll let them know. And if people deserve due credit, then I'll be really nice and do something extra special to please them. I do go out of my way for people, I really do. I try my best to please a lot of people. A lot of people notice that, when I'm on stage, I give my all. I give so much to the crowd, I try and give my best, because I want the crowd to know that I'm giving them their money's worth. I want to make them happy, and I want them to enjoy the show. I'm a very emotional person - I'll cry at sad movies - I'm very soft and very, very, very sensitive. So sensitive. Probably the most sensitive person in the band. If anyone says anything bad or negative about me, it really, really upsets me.

SHANE: I live one day at a time. I wake up in the morning and, honestly, I don't know where I'm going that day until I actually get there, or to the airport or wherever. I don't know what flight I'm going on. I don't know anything. I really don't. I'm really strange that way; it's not that I don't care, it's just that I don't want to have any worries. I don't want to know. It's just that when I get to where I've got to go, I'll do my thing - and that's the way I do it. I don't know what kind of a personality I have but I think, in general, I get on with anybody. I don't have problems with anybody, and if anybody has a problem with me then I don't bring that problem up. I just let it pass; I don't say anything. The problem flows over and I go on with life. I don't try to cause hassle for myself. I'll just let it go and on to the next thing. Am I reliable? As a mate, as a friend, yes - definitely. I'm trustworthy and I would do anything for anybody, that's for sure. I'm not moody. In fact, it takes quite a lot to get me going, to get in a row or anything. Unless people are going to argue about me being on time, because I'm not punctual at all!

RONAN: I guess I'm a fairly sensitive guy. I take time to listen to everybody and try my best to be on everybody's side. I don't like to take sides with anybody, but I'm fairly easy to read and people usually know where they stand with me. Also, I'm a good judge of people; I can tell what people are like. I like everything to run smoothly - which is very hard! I know what I'm about. I know what I want to do and what I'm trying to do. I don't like to take a step back and watch everything go by; I like to be involved in everything and know what's going on. I like to be involved in the musical side of things as much as I can - the production, the writing, the vocals...everything. The whole lot. I am an organised person, but not when it comes to hygiene and keeping things tidy. Just walk up to my room and you'll find out! Myself and Shane are the worst. Shane was a very clean person before he met me but, now, our room will be in bits! Clothes are everywhere. There are always three hotel rooms for Boyzone, and you'll know right away which one is mine and Shane's. I love it, though; I love being untidy when it comes to rooms. I know where everything is! I'm punctual, though - very punctual, too punctual - and I am moody. Everybody is. I try not to be too moody, though. I'll save the moodiness for myself, I don't like to show it to everybody else. I'm happy, though - very happy. Everybody gets unhappy from time to time, and I'm not going to say I don't, but I try to be as jolly and happy as I can. Having said that, if I don't get sleep - I'm an awful moan!

KEITH: I'd probably say, about myself, that when people first meet they think I'm a big, tough bad bloke. But, underneath all of that, when they get to know me they find out that I'm just a big softie, who would do anything for them. That's basically, from people coming back and talking to me about it, the image I put forward. People think I'm like a big, strong and arrogant person at times, but when they get to know me they realise that I'm a nice bloke and I'm quiet - and shy, sometimes. Apart from that, I am a messy bloke. In the morning times, a lot of the guys are cranky. Now, I have to be honest, I'm not one to be cranky in the mornings - unless I've been up all night - and, usually, when the boys are cranky I try and kind of cheer them up a bit by messing about and having a laugh. Sometimes I go too far trying to do it, and I cheese them off even more, but my heart is in the right place and I'm only trying to do what I can. The majority of the time I love messin' and having a laugh. It's just the way I

am - only, sometimes, I don't know when to stop! I like to think of myself as a good friend to my friends, as someone they can rely on through thick or thin. What else? I like having a good time and partying, and I'm not punctual. Not at all. I'm very, very bad. I'm probably the worst in the band in that respect. If anyone is to be late, it's usually me...

MIKEY: I think I'm of good character, and I would imagine I'm a good friend. I would do most anything for a friend. In fact, I would do anything for a good friend. I can be a little bit temperamental at times, I suppose, and probably impatient. I never used to be like that, actually; it wasn't until I came into the band that I became like that - I think because of the stress that's sometimes loaded on you. You can get a little bit hot under the collar from time to time. Equally, I never used to be particularly tidy before I joined the band - but now tidiness has become more of a thing to me. I think it's because I've become more independent. Being away from home all of the time, I've had to make a point of cleaning up my room. I don't like it to be in a dirty room, with clothes all over the place, I hate that - although my own room at home was like that for a while, because I was always only coming in and out and never had the time. Generally, I like a place to be clean - not like spick and span, I'm not fussy, by any means, but I like things clean. As for punctuality, I'd love to be on time all of the time...but I'm not. I have a great love affair with my bed, the greatest love affair of all time. I'd say I'm a fun-loving type of person, but you have to catch me on the right day. Humour and the way I mess around can sometimes be just an outside thing; underneath it all I'm a very, very deep person. I think an awful lot, sometimes I think too deeply about things for my own good. Like the big things don't bother me, but little things that wouldn't bother other people can sometimes depress me. You wouldn't imagine how deep I can be at times. I'm a very solitary person when the mood takes me. When I'm in that frame of mind, I need somebody - one of my good friends - to talk to. Like everybody, I suppose, and generally, a lot of young males, I found life confusing growing up. Love and all of that kind of stuff...when you're a child, it's kind of clean cut; you grow up, you fall in love, you get married and you have children. But, then, as you go through experience after experience you find out that it's not that way - and then you wonder why...

CAN'T STOP ME

In a group like Boyzone, hard work is par for the course. So what is it that motivates the guys in the group to keep going?

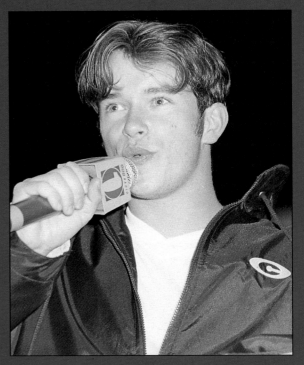

STEPHEN: My dream. The fact that all I've ever really wanted to do with my life, in the professional sense, is to be in a group and do the sort of things we're doing with Boyzone. It's a very rewarding life, in all senses, but you have to just grab it by the scruff of the neck and get on with it. As I've said, I do get homesick and I do get upset about being away, but it's the price you have to pay if you want things to happen for you - and it's not such a high price. I realise, as we all do, that everything we do is leading somewhere and pushing the band forward. At the same time, as you're progressing, you're also learning and travelling; finding out new things about yourself, the others in the band and about life in general. I'm also completely motivated by performing, and getting out on stage. For all of us, that is the ultimate thing about being in this band. The pleasure that I get from being in front of an audience and seeing that I am actually entertaining them, that people are getting visible joy out of what I'm doing, is fantastic. Unless you've experienced that for yourself, words can't really do it justice. This really is like a dream come true. I used to imagine what being in a successful group might be like before I joined Boyzone, and the truth of the matter is that the reality of it all is even more amazing than the fantasy. Living your dream is motivation enough for anybody.

SHANE: Completely what gets me going is driving. My head was wrecked when I had the broken ankle. I was really, really upset about being on stage on tour and not being able to dance with the guys and having to watch them while they were rehearsing, and I couldn't. I was very upset over that but, I think, what topped it all - because it's in my blood - was the fact that I couldn't drive. It just killed me. Cars, motorbikes...whatever, it's just in me. I have to have a car. Like, I'd have a car before a house. I'd live in a car! When I was a mechanic, I was basically working to pay for the car that I had. I went out to nightclubs with a fiver, just to get me into the club and dance, and that was it. I had no money because I was paying for petrol and so on, but that's what I wanted. That made me feel good, and that's what I lived for; my car. With me and cars, it's nothing to do with going fast at all - although, everywhere I go I sit in my car at 100mph. No, it's not even the speed; it's the fun. I wake up in the morning and I look out of the window to see if it's wet. I'm praying it's wet outside because, with a rear-wheel drive car, into corners and tailing is just...unreal. It's the best thing in the world. I just have to do it - and I'm probably going to get into a lot of trouble doing it, too. In town, in traffic, it doesn't matter where I am, the back of the car is always sideways up the road on every corner. The problem is, all my mates are the same. We all have rear-wheel drive cars for that particular reason. So there's four of us in a line, just sideways up the road. That's the way it is... Cars aside for a moment, so far as my career is concerned what motivates me is the idea of success. Of selling records, having hits and playing concerts. I always want to do things bigger and better - and, when it comes to Boyzone, I'm driven by the need to have people enjoy what we do. Knowing that our fans enjoy us and are entertained by us is really what this is all about. I suppose what also makes me tick is my attitude towards life. My favourite saying, and I think anyone who knows me would tell you this, is 'Stuff it!' (Editor's note: or words to that effect!) That is me all over. If something goes wrong - stuff it! I'll tell you, when I broke my ankle and I couldn't go on stage, I just said 'Stuff it - the show goes on.' D'you know what I mean? Stuff happens, and that's just the way it is.

● ● ● ● ● ● ● ● ● ● ● ● ● ● ● ● ● ●

RONAN: My Mum and Dad had to bring up five kids, and it was always very hard for them. I come from a comfortable family, but not a really, really wealthy one. It was always a job for my parents and it's made me feel really proud about what they've done for us. That's what drives me and motivates me. I'd like to do the same for my family. I don't have to struggle now. I will always work hard in my life, I know that, but I don't want to have to struggle in my life because this is a crazy world and it's a cut-throat world. People are knocked down like...that. On a personal level, I just want to be successful and I want to be respected as well. Respect is a big thing; people put you down and cut you down. I've seen pop acts come and go, and all I want is a bit of respect from people about my music, about our music. Maybe some day we'll get it. We get it now, but

there'll always be someone there to say 'You're only manufactured' or 'You're this and you're that.' Maybe one day people will really see the true side of Boyzone. Also, I'm motivated by something new, something different. Around every corner there's something different in this business. Every day is something different. Getting up on stage kind of makes me tick, too; watching the faces of the people as they're smiling and shouting. It's just an unbelievable sensation that goes through you. This is for us? Wow! Nobody can understand it - only us five guys and any other act that is or has been in the same position. But, like, us five guys when we get up there in front of an audience that is screaming and shouting...it's fantastic. The best feeling in the world. In those times, up on stage, you forget about all your worries about money and everything. Never mind about eating the right food or getting your sleep; you know that this is what you're there to do. This is what it's all about. Those are the things that get me going and drive me on to better myself and what we do as a band.

● ● ● ● ● ● ● ● ● ● ● ● ● ● ● ● ● ●

KEITH: What gets me going, and up in the morning? Basically, it's Mark Plunkett, our tour manager! No, seriously, because we work so hard and get very tired a lot of the time, sometimes when you're stuck in the middle of interviews, TV shows, radio shows...that's all part of the work, and we love it to bits, but sometimes the workload is so tough you forget what it's all about. When that starts to happen, we begin to have little rows among ourselves, we get run down and tired and we lose it for a little while. But as soon as we step on stage, just for the split second when we first step on the stage, then we say 'This is what it's all about'. The energy we get from the people, from the fans, is fantastic. The feeling you have inside because of it is something that only very few people can experience. It is just...overwhelming. It's completely amazing. That's what it's all about, and that's what makes me get out of bed in the morning.

● ● ● ● ● ● ● ● ● ● ● ● ● ● ● ● ● ●

MIKEY: I suppose it's just the fact of being alive, being able to get out of my bed in the morning. Being healthy enough that I can go about a day's work and be happy about that. Also, I'm getting up every morning that this band is together...and I'm fulfilling my dream.

PERSONAL FILES
MIKEY

● **FULL NAME:** Michael Christopher Charles Graham.

- **DATE OF BIRTH:** 15.8.72.

- **PLACE OF BIRTH:**
The Rotunda Hospital, Dublin.

- **BIRTHSIGN:** I'm a Leo, and I share every single one of my starsigns characteristics; I'm a strong type of person on the outside, but when it comes to affairs of the heart...I'm weak.

- **HOME:** Coolock, Dublin.

- **FAMILY:** Mum and Dad, Sheila and William, my eldest sister, Yvonne, 31, brother Niall, 30, Avril, 28, Catherine, 26, and then there's twins, Clare and Deborah, who are about 25. Then there's myself.

- **PREVIOUS JOBS:** Motor mechanic. But, before that, I had lots of part-time jobs. I was once a milkman, a lounge boy, a barman, a shop attendant in a supermarket, a porter in a large department store in Dublin. It was called Clearys, on O'Connell Street, and my father used to work there so he got me a job during the summer months.

- **SCHOOL DETAILS:** St. John Vianni Infants School, St. David's CBS Primary School, St. David's Christian Brothers School and then, finally, I began third level education at technical college studying motor mechanics. I was there for four years.

- **QUALIFICATIONS:** Leaving Certificate, which is equivalent to 'A' Levels. Fully qualified motor mechanic.

- **HEIGHT:** 5ft 8ins.

- **WEIGHT:** 10.5 to 11st.

- **SHOE SIZE:** 8.

- **FAVE NIGHT OUT:** To go out with family and friends and boogie on down, and maybe have a relaxing drink of hot chocolate when I go to the disco!

- **FAVE NIGHT IN:** To sit in, not that I get the chance or have anybody to sit in with, with someone special, a special girl maybe. I'd love that now, but if that's not available I'd just like to sit in by the fire on a winter's night, watch some videos and have lots of goodies in.

- **FAVE MOVIE:** Cool Hand Luke. There's a scene in it where the character played by Paul Newman eats loads of boiled eggs - and I have a bet with one of my friends, these last few years; he reckons that he can eat 50 boiled eggs in one hour, but he's not allowed to vomit any of them up. He hasn't managed it yet.

- **FAVE ACTOR:** Al Pacino.

- **FAVE ACTRESS:**
Meryl Streep is an excellent actress.

- **FAVE SONG:** 'One' by U2.

- **FAVE BAND:** The Police.

- **FAVE SINGER:** Sting.

- **FAVE ALBUM:** At the moment, it's the Beatles 'Blue' album; 1967-1970.

- **FAVE FOOD:** Pasta and chicken. It's a healthy meal, and I enjoy it.

- **FAVE DRINK:** Probably...Coke.

- **FAVE TV PROGRAMME:** I don't watch much TV, but probably The Cosbys or something like that.

- **FAVE COLOUR:** Black.

- **CAR:** A Mazda 626 2-litre injection.

- **HOBBIES:** I like to horse ride, I like water sports and, if I'm at a loose end, I like to get back in, messing about with cars - because I'm a mechanic by trade.

- **AMBITIONS:** The obvious one is to be successful, but I'm crazy about music and my ambition would be to do a duet with Sting because he's my idol as far as music is concerned.

COMING HOME NOW

Home is where the heart is, and home - for Boyzone - is Dublin, Ireland. They told us how they feel about their fair city, and about the others they now have to visit as their fame spreads around the globe and takes them away from the Emerald Isle.

STEPHEN

Being away and getting to see all these countries and all these beautiful cities is just amazing. All the wonderful scenery and the different people you meet, I wouldn't miss the experience for the world. My favourite city, so far, is Paris. Paris is just beautiful. I'm looking forward to going back there. But being away all the time can be very hard, on me more so than the rest of the guys. I think I can say that, and I think the guys will say that about me as well. I get really upset going away, and I get homesick very easily. Seeing all these beautiful countries, though, I say to myself 'Look what I'm seeing; I'm getting to see the world. I'm in a band...' I'd never flown anywhere before all of this. The first time I ever went on a plane was with Boyzone. We flew to London, I think it was to meet everyone at our record company, Polydor, over there. We went home the next day, so I didn't mind, but after that we had to go away for four days - and I was just crying. I was thinking 'I can't do this'. I used to cry a lot about leaving home. It was tough. Now it's pretty easy, although I still get homesick and I still do cry when I'm leaving home. It depends on how

long I'm leaving for. If it's five or six days, I can cope. If it's two weeks, I can't cope. It's too long for me. As for Dublin...I love Dublin so much, I really do. I'm going to live in Dublin. I'll die in Dublin, I will. Dublin is a great place. The people are great, they're friendly, and because it's a small city you really do feel at home there. I honestly love everything about it.

SHANE

When this band started and we started going to Britain and Europe and all of that, it was quite a big thing for us to leave home - and to get back home. Irish people are very homely. We're homely lads, we all still live with our Mas and Das...it's just a real homely thing. Because we started going away and we didn't see our families any more, we all got very homesick. We just had to get home every now and again. We still do have to, but I don't think it's half as much as we did. Dublin is a small city, and nothing can happen there without other people knowing. Like, you can walk down Dublin town and every second person, you'll say 'Hello' to. That's the way it is. Everybody knows everybody's business. It's like, not a big family as such, but...it's like when you go on holiday. You're in your holiday resort for two weeks, or whatever, and you get to know everybody. That's exactly the way it is back home in Dublin; you always know somebody when you go into town. Always. Before Boyzone, I had travelled. I'd been to Portugal quite a lot because my folks have a house over there - and the last holiday we all went on together, as a family, was to America for three weeks, to Disneyland and all that stuff, just because we knew it was going to be the last year together for a while - but now, seeing countries around the world, we're all beginning to realise that this is our job and this is why we're here. To go to other countries and to start to realise that not many other people get the chance to travel Europe or the world - be it a pop star or someone of any other profession. To actually get to do what we do, we're all starting to realise that not many people do it, and to make the most of it. It's amazing to go around other countries. And getting on an aeroplane now is just like getting on a bus and going into town. You do take it for granted, but it is really brilliant.

RONAN

Before Boyzone, I had travelled a bit. I'd been to New York, funnily enough, five months before the band was formed. I'd gone over to visit my brothers and sister in America, but I'd not really travelled much up to that point. Now, of course, there's no chance for my passport to collect any dust. We're travelling all the time. Initially, Boyzone was only really travelling around Europe - the UK, Belgium, Holland, Germany and places like that - but, of late, there seems to be a demand for us from further afield. As I'm being interviewed for this annual we're scheduled to go to Japan and South-East Asia for the first time. It's exciting. It's really, really exciting. I can't wait; the Far-East is one place I've always wanted to visit. I've always been influenced by the whole Far-East thing, so I'm really looking forward to going out there. I'm sure that will be an amazing experience and a chance for us all to see really different cultures. To be honest, it's a trip of a lifetime for us all. Of course, we will be working when we get out there - we must never forget that! - but the opportunity to go to these places at all is one which we're all extremely grateful for. As for Ireland, Ireland is very special to me. I mean, I've spent 18 years of my life in Ireland, and I'll spend another 18 - please God, another 50 - there. I love Ireland. It's a very warm country, a very beautiful country. I love it. It's just very special to the five of us. Dublin is a very small city, everybody knows everybody; there's no secrets in Dublin. The city seems to be very proud of us, which is very nice. We're always proud to go home. When we started up, a lot of people, a lot of the media, gave us a hard time. They put us down and said we were manufactured, but then we went home and accepted the National Entertainment Award for the 'Best New Act'. That just made us feel so proud. It made us feel that we could say to everybody 'We've made a stand. Here we are - we're in your face!' Then we accepted the IRMA Award in front of thousands of people in Ireland. That was another proud moment for us. Step by step, we're getting there. So to go home now is a good feeling.

KEITH

What Dublin and Ireland means to me is...home. Northside Dublin is my home, it's where I was born, where I was brought up and, basically, where I still live. It's where all my roots around my family are. Dublin is one of very few places left in the world - and I've been around the world, so I know this - where the people are very, very friendly. I'm not going to say that they're not begrudgers, because they are begrudgers and they begrudge an awful lot to you. Sometimes Dublin people can be very jealous, but that's not what I'm talking about.

What I'm talking about is the warmth of the place. For example, I think England is a great place, it opens up a lot of dreams for a lot of people, but it can be very cold at times because there's so many nationalities living under the same roof. I remember one day getting lost in London and I asked umpteen people the direction of where I was to go - and they just grunted at me, they wouldn't even answer me. Taxi drivers passed me by in the street. The only way I could actually get to where I was going to was to stop a police car. They brought me to Aldgate station and told me where to go, because I got totally lost. Dublin is not like that. If you got lost in Dublin and asked anybody on the street how to get where you wanted to go - they'd nearly bring you there themselves. Dublin is a very small place, but it's fulfilled. There's nothing that you want for in Dublin; there's plenty of fashion shops, plenty of clubs to go to a night, plenty of places to go during the day, places for kids... There's everything for everybody in such a small place. And everybody pretty much knows everybody else. It's a family. It's a lovely, lovely, lovely place and if you're brought up there and you live there, you really come to appreciate it when you have to live away from it. That's what Dublin and Ireland means to me. When I have to leave there, it's very, very hard at times because I have a lot of dear and special people to me in Dublin. I don't get to see an awful lot of them any more these days, so when I'm leaving I get very upset and I'm hurting inside because I'm going to miss them and not see them for a while. But it's my job, and I love it, and as soon as I get on that plane and arrive at the other country...as much as I love my family and everybody else, that goes out of my head. I'm there to enjoy myself and to do my job - and

that's exactly what I do. Before Boyzone, I'd only really travelled all over Ireland - and I'd been on a plane just twice. I saved up one summer, and I went away with to Greece with two of my friends on a holiday. It was the first holiday I ever had away from Ireland, and I never went away again after that until Boyzone. So Boyzone has given me the opportunity, that I probably never would have had otherwise, of seeing the whole of the world. And holidays now, since Boyzone, have brought me as far as North Africa. I wouldn't have had any of that, only for Boyzone. In the future we're going to places like China, Hong Kong...places I'd never have got to see. That's what Boyzone has done for me.

MIKEY

It's true that we do get to travel to a lot of places now, but there's a general attitude from some people that we're on holiday over there, or whatever. Some people are under the illusion that we just go to these places and completely relax. Instead, we work like...dogs! Out of all the countries we go to, if we get one day off in four - combining all the hours - then that's about the size of it. You might have an hour here and another hour there that, in total, equals a day. You don't really get to see the sights, the scenery or the nice parts of the places you visit, apart from through the bus window, because you're working by day and sleeping by night. As for Dublin, I love the place with all of my heart, and my heart is in Ireland, as such. It's a very closely-knit environment, where I come from, and the city itself - Dublin city - has a great togetherness you can feel; an atmosphere about it. Even down in the countryside, there's some of the most beautiful scenery in the world - and places where you can just sit back and you could stay there forever, for eternity, and nobody would come near you. Dublin has everything that anybody could want for; discos, shops, restaurants and places to relax. Boyzone has enabled us to travel everywhere, and we love doing that. We hate standing in Dublin airport and leaving, but once we get on the plane and then arrive at the other place we know that we'll be alright there. But the initial part of leaving Ireland, for that hour or so that you're standing in the airport, doesn't feel nice. And, you know, we're only human; sometimes it hits you when you're in a foreign country and you're lying in your bed at night, awake. You're heart is hurting and you feel, like, 'God - nothing is worth this...' But

then we realise that it's a chance in a lifetime to secure a great future for ourselves - while we're enjoying ourselves doing what we're doing. Eventually, when all of this quietens down, I will retire to Ireland. I will definitely settle down there. There's no doubt about it.

39

KEITH

● **FULL NAME:** Keith Peter Thomas Francis John Duffy.

● **DATE OF BIRTH:** 1.10.74.

● **PLACE OF BIRTH:**
The Rotunda Hospital, Dublin.

● **BIRTHSIGN:** Libra. I haven't a clue whether I'm typical of the starsign or not, because I don't know what a typical Libran is!..

● **HOME:** Dublin.

● **FAMILY:** Mum, Dad and two brothers.

● **PREVIOUS JOBS:** My first job was on a golf driving range, picking up all of the balls in the field. Then I worked in a bar as a barman. I was a waiter in a restaurant, and I worked in the kitchen. I was a bellboy in a hotel. I worked for more than 4 years in Frawleys department store. Then I worked in McKullus - Steve and I worked there together. Then I worked in numerous clubs as a doorman. I also worked all the major concerts in Ireland, and all the festivals like the Fleadh, as backstage and personal security to Neil Young and Van Morrison.

● **SCHOOL DETAILS:** My primary school was called Bellgrove National School, and the first secondary school I went to was Ard Scoil Reis, which is an Irish name. After that I went to Plunkett College and, from there, on to another college...which I can't remember the name of right now!

● **QUALIFICATIONS:** Various certificates.

● **HEIGHT:** 6ft 1in.

● **WEIGHT:** 13.5 to 14st.

● **SHOE SIZE:** 11.

● **FAVE NIGHT OUT:** Start off having a meal, a few glasses of wine, on to a club, dance all night, have a laugh - blah, blah, blah.

● **FAVE NIGHT IN:** Sitting in front of the telly, looking at a video with a Chinese meal.

● **FAVE MOVIE:**
Point Break, or an old film called Stripes.

● **FAVE ACTOR:** Robert De Niro.

● **FAVE ACTRESS:** Julie Roberts.

● **FAVE SONG:** Man In The Mirror by Michael Jackson.

● **FAVE BAND:** I don't really have a favourite band. I like all types of music, and there's loads of different bands whose music I really enjoy and listen to.

● **FAVE SINGER:** I don't really have one, again, but there was one particular song that I really loved when I was growing up; Unchained

Melody by The Righteous Brothers. I loved the way they sang that song, and I think they're amazing singers.

● **FAVE ALBUM:** I've had a few but, right now, it's Disc 1 of Michael Jackson's new album, HIStory.

● **FAVE FOOD:** Cabbage, potatoes and bacon. You can't beat it.

● **FAVE DRINK:** Budweiser.

● **FAVE TV PROGRAMME:** I don't get to see TV at all any more, but I used to love Neighbours.

● **FAVE COLOUR:** Blue.

● **CAR:** A Ford Escort RS.

● **HOBBIES:** Horse-riding, weight-training, swimming, go-karting...things like that.

● **AMBITIONS:** To continue to be successful, and to always be happy.

WHEN ALL IS SAID AND DONE

AND SO TO THE FUTURE; WHAT DO THE BOYS FROM BOYZONE WANT OUT OF LIFE AND THE SUCCESS WHICH THE GROUP HAS BROUGHT THEM?...

STEPHEN

I don't know! What am I doing this for? No, I'm getting to see the world. A lot of people of my age, where I come from, are just into drugs and a bad lifestyle. I just didn't want to see myself getting into that. I didn't want to see myself doing drugs, or robbing cars. I didn't want to see that. Down my area, where I live, there's a lot of that stuff going on. Luckily enough, I'll never see any of it. I don't want to see any of it. I know that the problems are there and I know that there's a lot to be done with the problems, but I don't want to be involved in problems like that. I love the band, and I'll go on with the band, and I'll try to make people as happy as I can. In life, in general, there's a lot of things I still want to do. I want to see the rest of the world, I want to settle down and have a house. I would love a house. My main ambition in life is to have a house and happiness, and just be able to do what I want to do and go where I want to go - not have other people saying 'Be here at that time and there at this time.' I know it's hard, being in the band in that respect. People do say to you 'Right, you've got to do this interview', or whatever. Which is grand, like, I mean we don't mind doing interviews, for example. It's great fun at times and it gives us a break, so that we can relax. But me, personally, what I'm looking forward to is that day that'll come where I'll be able to make my own decisions and my own choices in what I want to do and where I want to go. And that could be far away, but I'll live with that - that's grand - because I love the band and I love what I do. Without the band, I'm nothing. Without the band, what would I be? Where would I be? Without the fans, where would I be? They're there to meet you at the

airport, and so on. At the moment, though, the band is my life. It is my life. And I love it for that reason. I enjoy everything about it - we have great laughs at interviews, in videos - it's all fun. It's hard work, but there's a lot of fun and a lot of enjoyment involved. That, in life, is very important; to enjoy yourself and have fun. I know that, in the future, I'm still going to have fun and still going to have a life - and I'll be with the guys all the time. These guys are going to be my best mates for life. Apart from any of that, I just want a house and to be happy. And I'll do this forever. Even if the band does end, I'm going to continue in music - whether it be writing or producing for bands, or singing. I just want to be in this business. I love acting, as well... I love the entertainment business; I don't think I could live without it.

SHANE

Mainly, when I was growing up as a kid, I got a lot of hassle out of being a 'poser', and what have you. Not that I was; I think it was because I was, you know, a good-looking chap. The last thing I was was a poser, and that's being quite honest. I was no more vain than I was anything else. I'd go to school mucked up to the eyeballs after being on my motorbike. That was me all over; I'd get out of bed, put on my clothes and go to school - and I wouldn't care what way my hair was. It still didn't matter, though; I was a poser, and that was the way people thought of me. Because of that, I always knew that I was going to be one up from everybody else. I knew I was going to have money, drive a Porsche... Don't know how I thought I was going to do it, because I didn't do anything in school, but I did. I always knew that I was going to come out top dog and land on my feet when I got out of school. And I did. So, definitely, for me that was an achievement that I wanted to succeed in. Just to say 'Stuff the lot of you'. Everybody around my area had a thing about me. I suppose it had something to do with women, too. I'm sure that they dislike me even more now, but I'm glad I've got where I am and got to this stage so that I

can just say 'Stuff everybody.' It's a good feeling. As for the future, most definitely I will have a family. A wife and, say, four kids. I want to live in a house in a forestry kind of area with a nice lake or a river at the back garden - with a speedboat. That is me. That is just me, you know? Through the forest there's a nice scrambling track for my motorbike. That is me all over. I'm 19 now, and I'd like to go for the wife and kids in about seven years, but I've got to live a life for myself first.

KEITH

Boyzone, for us all, is an opportunity to make something of ourselves and our lives. I believe that's the way we all view it, and I know that we're all completely committed to working hard and to doing whatever is necessary to make the group as successful as it could possibly be. When all is said and done, that's what this whole thing is all about. We're fortunate to find ourselves in this position, but we're not taking any of it for granted. It could all disappear just as quickly as it arrived. Like Keith, I come from the same background. There was, like, seven kids in my family and we never wanted for anything. We always had everything that we needed - especially lots of love surrounding us. But I want to work really, really hard now and secure a future for myself, my future wife and children. If that works out, that's excellent but, at the end of the day, once I have happiness then I couldn't ask for more.

MIKEY

When this is all over - please God that never happens, because it's my dream, it's my life - but when it is all over, I would like to settle down, get married, have about five or six kids, live comfortably for the rest of my life, never have to worry about money and generally, basically, just be totally happy. And if I want to bring my kids and my wife away on a holiday, have the money to do that. If I want to buy my kids a bike, have the money to do that. Just live comfortably. I come from a working background, and I've seen my mother and father struggle. We've always had a wonderful house, and everybody was always welcome in it, but I remember growing up and going to school and having kids there say 'My mummy and daddy are rich - and they have this and they have that', and I never knew how to reply to that. I remember going home from school one day and saying to my mother 'Mummy? Are we rich?' And she said 'Yes, we are rich. But we're not rich in money - we're rich in love.' I know now what she was talking about, and that's the sort of family I've come from. I've seen them struggle from time to time, like coming to Christmas, having three kids and trying to get them all the pressies they want. Basically, all I want is the exact same kind of family that I come from, but to have a bit more money so we don't have to struggle. I never wanted for anything as a child, I always got what I wanted, but my mother and father had to work hard for it. I'm working hard now, but I'd like to just sit back in later years and enjoy my kids, enjoy my wife and have a good life together.

RONAN

When all is said and done, pop acts don't last forever, and everybody knows that. But maybe we'd like to progress on, and we'll stay in the pop industry for as long as we can. Maybe we could progress into another age group and remain in the music business. We might become... Manzone! You never know. But I love the guys, and it would break my heart if we would ever have to split up, so I don't like to think about that. We're five talented guys - there's no reason why we should split up or not continue in the music industry. We'll just have to see what happens. For myself, in the future I suppose I'd like all of those things that everyone else wants out of life. I'd like a wife, a family of my own, a nice house...security and peace of mind. Fortunately for me, I'm in a position where I'm doing a job in an industry which could bring me all of the things I'd like from a financial point of view. But, obviously, money

and material things is only a part of life. It's actually more important to me that I'm happy as a person.

That I feel fulfilled and get satisfaction out of what I'm doing with my life. I'm lucky that this job is my chosen career. It's what I wished I would be able to do with my life, long before it actually came to be. Personally, I've always wanted to be in a pop act. I've always been interested in music. I was in two rock bands before, but for me to get into Boyzone was just unbelievable. For me, it was every dream I ever had come true. I've got to see a lot of the world so far and, please God, I'll get to see more of it. I feel very proud to be in the band with the other four guys because they're great guys, and I've made four very good friends - which is very hard in a lifetime. You meet one good friend usually in a lifetime, if you're lucky. I've met four. We're five brothers...!